D1714157

HOW TO PLAY

If it's your book you can decide who plays first, or if it' s your house you can decide.

Or maybe, you can toss a coin, arm-wrestle, or go a few rounds of 'rock-paper- scissors'.

Whatever method you choose it's likely that someone will get upset, so let's all move on and let them go first.

It's all about having fun and no one wants to listen to a cry-baby.

The player who has to answer the question, has to justify his answer in a funny way,

There is no right or wrong answer, the main thing is that it is as hilarious as possible

You can decide to nominate one or more arbitrators, if you are more than two people, who will judge the hilarity or not of the justification.

If your answer is juged funny by the arbitrator or the majority of arbitrators, in this case you get a point, otherwise you get a nice little zero.

You will take turns playing until you decide to quit, and then you will calculate each player's points.

Whoever has the most, wins the game.

Remember, winning is great, it's even awesome, but the most Important thing is to have a good time !!!

Enjoooy !!!

WOULD YOU RATHER ?

go trick or treating

- Or -

go out on a date?

have a creative costume

- Or -

a scary costume?

WOULD YOU RATHER?

eat candy apple

- Or -

candy corn?

go to a real haunted house

- Or -

watch a horror movie marathon?

WOULD YOU RATHER ?

be absolutely terrified of the dark

- Or -

be afraid of the the thing underneath your bed?

have a Halloween party

- Or -

a Christmas party?

WOULD YOU RATHER ?

Visit a cemetery

- Or -

Visit a pet cemetery at midnight?

Watch a scary movie with a scary movie buff

- Or -

Watch a scary movie with a scaredy cat?

WOULD YOU RATHER ?

eat candy every day for a month

- Or -

have no candy for a month?

eat candy corn

- Or -

marshmallows?

WOULD YOU RATHER ?

go trick or treating
as a kid

- Or -

as an adult with your
kids?

get attacked by a giant
spider

- Or -

a spooky skeleton?

WOULD YOU RATHER ?

give out candy

- Or -

take candy?

risk getting tricked

- Or -

give our king sized candies
all night?

WOULD YOU RATHER ?

visit a haunted house

- Or -

a haunted graveyard?

be scared

- Or -

make someone else scared?

WOULD YOU RATHER ?

have candy for dinner

- Or -

have candy for
breakfast?

be a real-life Vampire

- Or -

Werewolf?

WOULD YOU RATHER ?

trick or treat in your neighborhood

- Or -

a different neighborhood?

go trick or treating with a group of friends

- Or -

with a group of family members?

WOULD YOU RATHER ?

eat candy corn

- Or -

smarties?

be chased by Friday
the 13th's Jason

- Or -

Halloween's Michael?

WOULD YOU RATHER ?

be a black cat

- Or -

a vampire bat?

drink apple juice

- Or -

eat pumpkin spice cake?

WOULD YOU RATHER ?

be locked in a room
full of snakes

- Or -

rats?

dress up as a character
from Harry Potter

- Or -

Star Wars?

WOULD YOU RATHER ?

explore a corn maze

- Or -

a haunted house?

face a Zombie Apocalypse

- Or -

an Invasion of 10-ft spiders?

WOULD YOU RATHER ?

live a world where
King Kong

- Or -

megalodon are real?

trick or Treat in
a *store-bought*

- Or -

homemade costume?

WOULD YOU RATHER ?

be given a Snicker's Bar

- Or -

a Reese's Peanut
But cup?

be forced to eat
lobster brains

- Or -

alligator hearts Fear
Factor style?

WOULD YOU RATHER?

never celebrate
Halloween

- Or -

thanksgiving again?

put "I'll Be Back"

- Or -

"I Told You I Was Sick"
on your gravestone?

WOULD YOU RATHER ?

have a nightmare
featuring the clown
Pennywise

- Or -

the Headless
Horseman?

have vampire teeth

- Or -

a witch's mole on
your nose?

WOULD YOU RATHER ?

eat pumpkin pie

- Or -

apple donuts?

stay at the Hotel Transylvania

- Or -

the Monster House?

WOULD YOU RATHER?

eat a caramel apple

- Or -

a caramel popcorn ball?

light a bonfire

- Or -

a candle at the graves of the dead?

WOULD YOU RATHER ?

see a UFO

- Or -

Bigfoot?

carve a jack-o-lantern

- Or -

play some pranks?

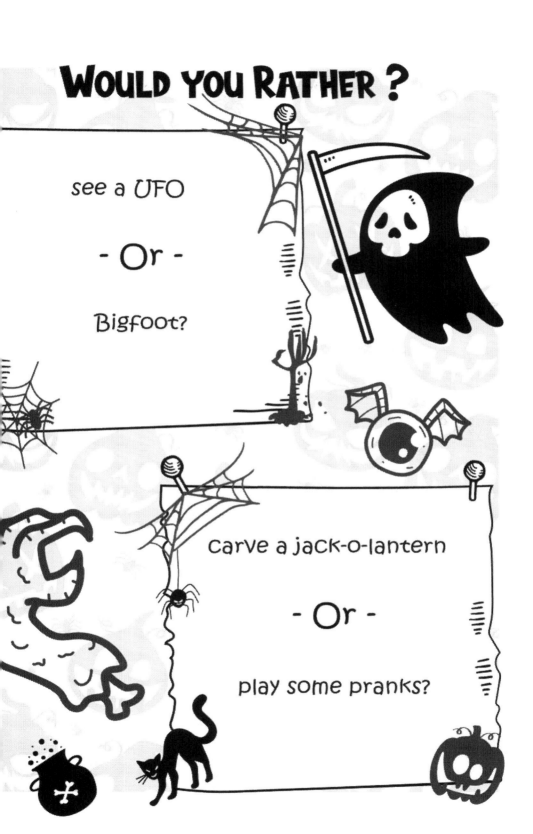

WOULD YOU RATHER ?

ride the Tower
of Terror

- Or -

the Haunted Mansion?

watch Beetlejuice

- Or -

Ghostbusters?

WOULD YOU RATHER ?

meet a vampire

- Or -

meet a werewolf?

get a surprise visit from Frankenstein's monster

- Or -

surprise visit from The Headless Horseman?

WOULD YOU RATHER?

walk through a graveyard at midnight

- Or -

pend a night in a spooky abandoned old house?

dunk for apples

- Or -

carve a jack-lantern?

WOULD YOU RATHER ?

go trick or treating

- Or -

stay home and watch
a scary movie?

be a ghost

- Or -

a zombie?

WOULD YOU RATHER ?

be dressed up as Superman/Wonder Woman

- Or -

as Batman / Catwoman?

spend Halloween night at a haunted house

- Or -

spend the night at a cemetery?

WOULD YOU RATHER ?

only eat chocolate

- Or -

only eat gummy candies for the rest of your life?

be able to transform into a bat

- Or -

a black cat?

WOULD YOU RATHER ?

want to have a
werewolf as a friend

- Or -

have a vampire as
a friend?

sleep in a room full of
spiders

- Or -

sleep in a room full of
snakes?

WOULD YOU RATHER ?

eat a whole raw onion

- Or -

eat a clove of garlic?

walk through a dark
forest on your own

- Or -

walk through a dark
graveyard on your own?

WOULD YOU RATHER ?

watch a scary movie

- Or -

watch a funny movie?

play a prank on your siblings

- Or -

play a prank on your parents?

WOULD YOU RATHER ?

carve 20 pumpkins

- Or -

eat 10 bags of candy corn?

meet a werewolf

- Or -

a zombie?

WOULD YOU RATHER ?

be wrapped up like a mummy for one hour

- Or -

lie in a closed coffin for one hour?

be Covered in spiders

- Or -

snakes?

WOULD YOU RATHER?

read horror stories

- Or -

watch horror movies?

live in a zombie apocalypse

- Or -

post-nuclear war?

WOULD YOU RATHER ?

have nightmares about
Freddy Krueger

- Or -

Jason Voorhees?

be a zombie

- Or -

a vampire?

WOULD YOU RATHER ?

make your own costume

- Or -

buy one from a store?

have curly red hair

- Or -

long black hair?

WOULD YOU RATHER ?

be a horror movie hero

- Or -

villain?

have a pet bat

- Or -

a spider?

WOULD YOU RATHER ?

go trick-or-treating
with your friends

- Or -

get paid to take a kid
trick-or-treating?

carve 5 giant pumpkins

- Or -

50 small ones?

WOULD YOU RATHER ?

put your hand in a tank
full of spiders

- Or -

a tank full of snakes?

have it rain candy corn

- Or -

sneakers?

WOULD YOU RATHER ?

win a contest for carving the best jack-o-lantern

- Or -

win best costume?

go to a pumpkin patch

- Or -

grow your own pumpkin?

WOULD YOU RATHER ?

sacrifice yourself to save your family

- Or -

live and have them die?

fly on a witch's broom

- Or -

drink some witch's brew?

WOULD YOU RATHER ?

go trick-or-treating
with a vampire

- Or -

a zombie?

visit a haunted house

- Or -

an abandoned
cemetery?

WOULD YOU RATHER ?

sleep in a coffin

- Or -

inside a giant pumpkin?

sleep in a coffin

- Or -

in a haunted house?

WOULD YOU RATHER ?

make a haunted house

- Or -

go to an actual haunted house?

wear a princess costume

- Or -

a minion outfit?

WOULD YOU RATHER?

eat a frog

- Or -

fish eyeballs?

spend a night in a haunted house

- Or -

haunt a house yourself?

WOULD YOU RATHER ?

at a bloody Snickers bar

- Or -

a Twix covered in underarm hair and sweat?

enjoy eating all your Halloween candies

- Or -

exchange all of them for $15?

WOULD YOU RATHER ?

be chased by Zombies

- Or -

wolves?

go trick-or-treating
in the mall

- Or -

in your neighborhood?

WOULD YOU RATHER ?

et bitten by a werewolf

- Or -

a vampire?

Only watch horror movies

- Or -

never be able to see
movies again?

WOULD YOU RATHER ?

get to trick

- Or -

treat?

get dressed as an angel

- Or -

a devil?

WOULD YOU RATHER ?

have a pumpkin for
a head

- Or -

have skeleton hands?

eat all of your Halloween
candy right away

- Or -

only eat one candy
every day for a year?

WOULD YOU RATHER ?

fall into a pool of blood

- Or -

kiss a monster?

stay home to give out candy

- Or -

go trick-or-treating?

WOULD YOU RATHER ?

want to be a superhero

- Or -

a villain for Halloween?

go trick or treating with your friends

- Or -

watch a scary movie at home with your friends?

WOULD YOU RATHER ?

be able to fly on a broomstick

- Or -

have a magic wand?

have Halloween just once a year

- Or -

all year round?

WOULD YOU RATHER ?

wear something that makes it impossible to walk

- Or -

wear something too tight that you can hardly breathe?

have a pumpkin for a head

- Or -

pumpkins as feet?

WOULD YOU RATHER ?

be super sweaty in your onesie costume on a warm Halloween night

- Or -

out in your tiny/thin costume on a cold Halloween night?

visit a haunted trail

- Or -

be the one haunting people?

WOULD YOU RATHER ?

be in a zombie apocalypse

- Or -

a ghost in a school forever?

wear a scary costume

- Or -

dress as a baby?

WOULD YOU RATHER ?

feel sick from too much
candy

- Or -

not have any candy
at all?

have all your pumpkins
smashed

- Or -

get egged?

WOULD YOU RATHER ?

have a ghost hiding in
your closet

- Or -

a scary clown?

go for a week with only
hooting like an owl

- Or -

only talking with your
mouth full of candy
corn?

WOULD YOU RATHER ?

have to spend the night in a coffin

- Or -

empty the insides of a 50 lb pumpkin using only your hands?

eat an entire pumpkin pie

- Or -

drink a gallon of green Halloween juice?

WOULD YOU RATHER ?

going to school wearing a pumpkin on your head

- Or -

dressed as a mummy?

spend Halloween eating as much candy as you wish

- Or -

scaring as many friends as you want?

WOULD YOU RATHER ?

wear a costume with an itchy wig

- Or -

a costume with fake teeth?

eat a pound of raw pumpkin seeds

- Or -

a pound of tootsie rolls?

WOULD YOU RATHER ?

eat a raw onion

- Or -

a clove of garlic?

to sleep in a graveyard on Halloween night

- Or -

in a haunted house?

WOULD YOU RATHER ?

eat only candy corn

- Or -

only "fun-sized" candy bars
for an entire month?

be covered in pumpkin
guts

- Or -

in vampire blood?

WOULD YOU RATHER ?

sing the National Anthem for one of this weekend's football games

- Or -

operate the scoreboard?

be able to say "Trick or Treat" in every language in the world

- Or -

know the answer to 500 Trivial Pursuit questions?

WOULD YOU RATHER ?

be a werewolf

- Or -

a vampire?

march in a Halloween parade in your town in a toddler-sized costume

- Or -

be pulled in the parade in a wagon covered in silly string?

WOULD YOU RATHER ?

see your name on a tombstone in your town's graveyard

- Or -

your name on the mailbox outside of a haunted house?

be able to eat as much as your want but not be able to taste your Halloween candy

- Or -

only be able to eat a little bit but have it taste perfectly yummy?

WOULD YOU RATHER ?

have to wear your Halloween costume every day for a month

- Or -

a suit of candy corn for one day?

have to open 1000 Double Bubble gum wrappers

- Or -

bake 100 Halloween cookies?

WOULD YOU RATHER ?

meet a vampire on Halloween

- Or -

a mummy?

be stuck in a home that has no power on Halloween

- Or -

in a house that has no candy?

WOULD YOU RATHER ?

eat your whole dinner
with no utensils

- Or -

have to eat dinner
served inside a
carved-out pumpkin?

not be allowed to speak
on Halloween

- Or -

not be allowed to
have candy?

WOULD YOU RATHER ?

have to invite your teacher to go trick or treating with you

- Or -

spend Halloween handing out candy at a classmate's house that you don't know very well?

have bright orange hair

- Or -

dark brown teeth?

WOULD YOU RATHER ?

go forward in time and enjoy trick or treating with your family 50 years in the future

- Or -

back in time and enjoy trick or treating with your family from 50 years ago?

live in the woods in a haunted house for a year

- Or -

at the International Space Station for a year?

WOULD YOU RATHER ?

spend Halloween in
a home without
electricity

- Or -

in a home without
running water?

run into a real zombie
on Halloween

- Or -

a real vampire?

WOULD YOU RATHER ?

be invited to the White House for Halloween night

- Or -

have a celebrity come to your house to hand out Halloween candy with you?

go swimming in a dark pond all alone on Halloween night

- Or -

have to walk through a spider-infested forest all alone to get home?

WOULD YOU RATHER ?

only be able to whisper

- Or -

only be able to shout
everything you say
on Halloween?

have to wear fangs all day
on Halloween

- Or -

carry around a
broomstick?

WOULD YOU RATHER ?

have the powers of a superhero on Halloween

- Or -

a ghost's ability to terrify your friends?

have a constant itch

- Or -

have constant hiccups while trick or treating?

WOULD YOU RATHER ?

have a costume malfunction in public

- Or -

an allergic reaction to your face paint?

wear an incredibly itchy wig all night

- Or -

super uncomfortable fake teeth all night?

WOULD YOU RATHER ?

see the costumes at a Halloween dog parade

- Or -

human parade?

Voldemort crashed your sleepover

- Or -

Darth Vader?

WOULD YOU RATHER ?

hand out candy to
trick-or-treaters

- Or -

ignore trick-or-treaters
and watch horror
movies all night?

go to a Halloween party

- Or -

go Trick or Treating?

WOULD YOU RATHER ?

go trick or treating with an embarrassing parent

- Or -

an embarrassing teacher?

get your groove on to "Thriller"

- Or -

boogie down to "Monster Mash"?

WOULD YOU RATHER ?

walk through cobwebs

- Or -

walk over eyeballs?

meet a witch

- Or -

meet a ghost?

WOULD YOU RATHER ?

have to clean you your house after it's been toilet papered

- Or -

your car after it's been egged?

get caught stealing all of the candy from an unguarded bowl on Halloween

- Or -

get bit by a big hairy spider?

WOULD YOU RATHER ?

go to a pumpkin patch

- Or -

go to an apple orchard?

be chased by a zombie

- Or -

be chased by frankenstein?

WOULD YOU RATHER ?

read a spooky book

- Or -

watch a spooky movie?

have candy corn for teeth

- Or -

be wrapped up like a mummy?

WOULD YOU RATHER ?

be able to fly on a witch's broomstick

- Or -

be invisible like a ghost?

eat one piece of candy a day until you run out

- Or -

eat all your candy in one night?

WOULD YOU RATHER?

eat candy corn

- Or -

eat candy/caramel apples?

eat pumpkin pie

- Or -

eat pumpkin bread?

WOULD YOU RATHER ?

go trick or treating

- Or -

pass out candy to trick or treaters?

ride a broomstick around everywhere you go for 1 week

- Or -

only be able to walk like a zombie for 1 week?

WOULD YOU RATHER ?

paint a pumpkin

- Or -

carve a pumpkin?

get only chocolat candy

- Or -

get only gummy candy?

WOULD YOU RATHER ?

wear only orange to school the whole week of halloween

- Or -

wear only black to school the whole week of halloween?

have a spooky black cat for a pet

- Or -

have a spooky bat for a pet?

WOULD YOU RATHER ?

wear a pumpkin on your
head for 1 day
to school

- Or -

wear vampire teeth at
school for 1 week?

sit by frankenstein on the
school bus

- Or -

sit by a vampire ont
the school bus?

WOULD YOU RATHER ?

share your Halloween candy with your parents

- Or -

your friends?

put your hand in a bowl of pumpkin guts

- Or -

a bowl of green jello?

WOULD YOU RATHER ?

eat as candy as you want on Halloween

- Or -

only get one piece of candy a day until its gone?

have to carry a pumpkin with you everywhere you go all day

- Or -

wear a witch nose with a wart all day long?

WOULD YOU RATHER ?

live in a giant pumpkin

- Or -

live in a haunted house?

hang upside down
to sleep

- Or -

sleep in a coffin?

WOULD YOU RATHER ?

tell your friends what you're going to be for Halloween

- Or -

or keep it secret until Halloween night?

get bags full of random candy

- Or -

get 1 bag of your favorite candy?

WOULD YOU RATHER ?

spend the night in a haunted house

- Or -

have a zombie for a sleepover at your house?

get attacked by a giant spider

- Or -

a spooky skeleton?

WOULD YOU RATHER?

decorate one giant pumpkin

- Or -

10 tiny pumpkins?

dress up as a spooky cat

- Or -

a spooky dog?

WOULD YOU RATHER ?

eat all of your halloween sweets

- Or -

trade your sweets in for 10$?

stroke a witch's cat

- Or -

cuddle a slimy frog?

WOULD YOU RATHER ?

be terrified of the dark

- Or -

be afraid of the thing under your bed?

eat slugs for dinner

- Or -

eat snails for breakfast?

WOULD YOU RATHER ?

pee your pants every time you are scared on Halloween

- Or -

faint?

have to sit next to someone in class wearing a gory mask

- Or -

someone who lets out a blood-curling scream every ten minutes?

WOULD YOU RATHER ?

have to howl like a werewolf and run on all fours s you race around a high school track

- Or -

roll a 25 lb pumpkin around a high school track?

have to say everything you are thinking

- Or -

never be able to speak at all on Halloween?

WOULD YOU RATHER ?

go trick or treating in your neighborhood

- Or -

trick or treating at the mall?

be invisible

- Or -

be able to move through walls?

WOULD YOU RATHER ?

go without TV and internet on Halloween

- Or -

have to watch scary movies nonstop on Halloween?

have to write a spooky story for Halloween

- Or -

make a scary movie?

Made in the USA
Columbia, SC
12 October 2021